Elf~help for
Dealing with
Difficult People

Elf~help for Dealing with Difficult People

written by
Lisa O. Engelhardt

illustrated by
R.W. Alley

ONE
CARING
PLACE

Abbey Press

Text © 2002 by Lisa O. Engelhardt
Illustrations © 2002 by St. Meinrad Archabbey
Published by One Caring Place
Abbey Press
St. Meinrad, Indiana 47577

Library of Congress Catalog Number
2002103653

ISBN 978-0-87029-366-5

Printed in the United States of America

Foreword

"She is so pushy!" "He lives in la-la land." "I can't stand it when somebody is two-faced!" "They must be punctuality-challenged." "If you weren't so wishy-washy, you'd take a stand on this." "He doesn't do a thing to help and then hogs all the glory."

Some people are just plain difficult—or, at least, we have difficulty dealing with them. They get on our nerves and bring out our worst. We spend inordinate amounts of time and energy wrestling with the anger they arouse in us.

We can't avoid life's "bad guys"—we live, work, socialize, and share public places with them. Telling them off is almost always counterproductive, as is holding a grudge. What recourse do we have?

Enter the little elves in this book. Follow their footsteps to learn what works and what doesn't work in dealing with the villains in your life. Along the way, you'll pick up some tips on appreciating differences and exploring your own "shadow side." With a bit of practice, you'll be empowered to bring peace and harmony to your problem relationships.

...And, yes, you could just casually leave this little book lying around. Perhaps a certain "difficult person" will benefit from it too!

1.

When people rub us the wrong way, it causes friction—at home, on the road, across the cubicles, in the bleachers.
For the sake of inner peace and the communal good, we need to find a way to deal with difficult people.

2.

With divine wisdom, imagination, and humor, the Creator cast each one of us as an individual. "Different" is sometimes "difficult" to understand. Remember, you are different too!

3.

Explore your own personality type and usual style of thinking and acting, as well as others'. Appreciate the interesting, valuable differences among you.

4.

Each of us looks at the world out of our own mindset. But none of us is the "norm"—the poster person for perfect conduct or the exemplar of excellence. Keep an open mind.

5.

If we repeatedly have the same difficulty with people, we need to consider whether we are somehow contributing to it. Ask a good friend to help you identify behavior on your part that may be problematic.

6.

We often dislike in others what we reject in ourselves. What parts of yourself do you have trouble accepting? Befriend this "shadow side" of yourself.

7.

You are not what someone else decides you are. As Eleanor Roosevelt has said, "No one can make you feel small without your consent." Don't buy into someone's mistaken judgment of you.

8.

Every time an aggravating person pops into your head, pray: "God bless you, _____."
Wish that person well. Pray, too, for yourself—for patience, understanding, and compassion.

9.

Accept the truth that, no matter how good of a person you are, some people will never understand you or like you—sometimes for reasons that have nothing to do with you at all.

10.

Ask yourself: Will this conflict matter five years from now? How much energy do I want to invest in it? What would happen if I just let it go?

11.

Give the benefit of the doubt. Is this person having a bad day or going through a tough time? Could there be some misunderstanding? Is this the first incident or have there been others?

12.

If the offensive behavior occurs only occasionally, you may want to step back and give the person a little latitude. If the behavior is chronically bothersome, then you probably need to take steps toward addressing it.

13.

Talking with a friend about a difficult person can help defuse anger and offer an objective view. But don't let such discussion take the place of working things out with the actual person.

14.

Try to avoid demonizing your antagonist. No one is either a saint or a devil. Don't poison others' opinions about the difficult person. They may see redeeming qualities that you cannot.

15.

It's much easier to judge, badmouth, and believe in our own moral superiority than to confront a difficult person constructively. Summon your courage and take the high road.

16.

Focus on the problem, rather than the person. Try not to judge or analyze character or motivation. It's not up to us to reform other people or improve their character.

17.

The biblical admonition to "turn the other cheek" does not mean we should continually overlook hostile, abusive, or threatening behavior. It is possible to assert your rights in a loving way.

18.

Being afraid of another's anger gives that person power over you. Each of us is responsible for his own anger, however. You cannot "make" someone else angry. Withstand the blast, if necessary, and control your own temper.

19.

Ask before you accuse. What you feel is an attack may simply be a misunderstanding. Since no one can read another's mind or motive, don't assume malice. There may be a simple explanation you have overlooked.

20.

Speak gently, from your heart, saying only what you know to be true—the facts and your feelings about them. Blaming, accusing, or using abusive language will only put the other person on the defensive.

21.

State simply, directly,
and calmly:

When you _____,
I feel _____,
because _____.
What can we do about this?

22.

If you feel yourself getting out of control, count to 10 (or 1000, if need be). Breathe deeply to regain your composure. If you still feel that positive communication is not possible, postpone further discussion till later.

23.

Remember…It's not as important to prove that you are "right," as to behave rightly. The goal is not to dominate or defeat, but to arrive at a mutually acceptable solution.

24.

Really listen to the other person's point of view. People are much more likely to be receptive to change if they first feel understood.

25.

Some people cannot or will not deal with you in good faith, no matter how respectfully you approach them. You cannot change others—only yourself. Consider what alternative courses of action are available to you.

26.

Once you've said your piece,
make peace with it.
Congratulate yourself for
exercising courage and control.

27.

If the other person was not receptive, hope for a better outcome after he has had time to think it over. It may take several encounters to help him understand the issue and agree to work toward a solution.

28.

If you suspect a physical, mental, or emotional problem may be at the root of the problem, speak in confidence with someone who can help.

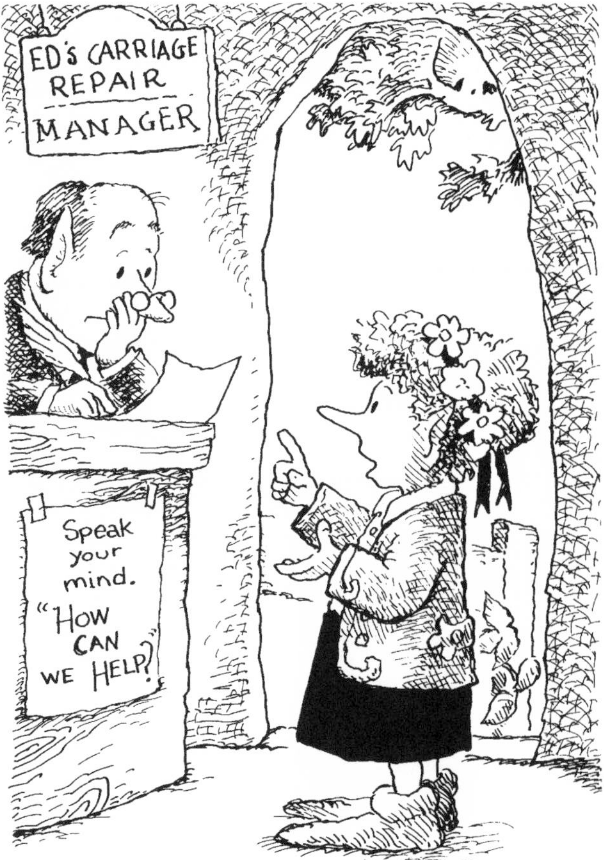
ED's CARRIAGE REPAIR
MANAGER
Speak your mind. "HOW CAN WE HELP?"

29.

We need to set clear boundaries with some people to protect ourselves from further injury. Firmly state what behavior is off-limits and enforce this.

30.

Try to put aside your own very human desire to return hurt for hurt. Whenever we suffer injury and do not respond in kind, we rid the world of that much evil.

31.

It's fitting to talk about "carrying" a grudge, for bearing ill will is indeed a heavy burden. Let go of a grudge and feel a huge weight lift off your shoulders.

32.

Forgiveness is one of the hardest things on earth to do in the face of irritation, intimidation, or hostility. That's why we need heaven's help. Pray to forgive.

33.

The word "FREES" is hidden in
the word "FoRgivEnEsS."
Forgiving frees the forgiver—
from rage and resentment.
Forgive and go free.

34.

Forgiveness is not instantaneous. It's a many-layered process, as we gradually let go of hurt, pride, and bitterness. The Bible says to forgive "seventy-seven times"— maybe even for the same injury.

35.

We can obsess over a difficult
relationship so much that we
create a destructive spiral of
rage, overreaction, and stress.
Take time each day to center
yourself and renew your spirit.

36.

Discharge excess adrenaline with exercise or your favorite form of relaxation. Try to obliterate the problem from your mind for twenty-four hours. Give your stress a rest.

37.

"Difficult" people may be
God's way of teaching us
patience, tolerance, and loving
assertiveness. Stretch your
heart and grow.

38.

God knows it's hard to deal
with some people. Yet God is
with us in our struggles, giving
us the courage to work toward
change and the serenity to
accept the outcome.